X3   9/05

D0116484

X3   9/05

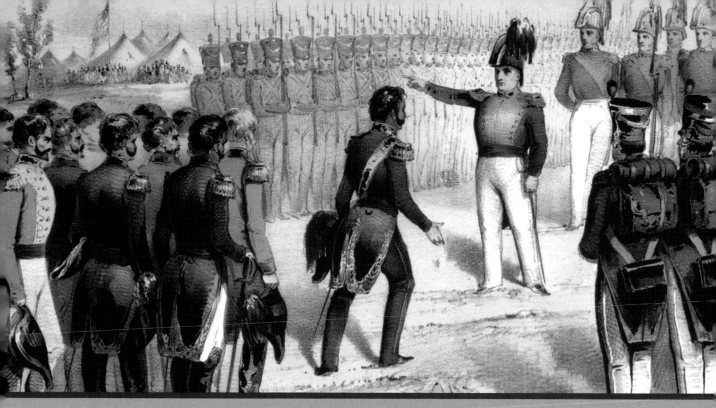

THE MEXICAN-AMERICAN WAR

A PRIMARY SOURCE HISTORY OF THE EXPANSION OF THE WESTERN LANDS OF THE UNITED STATES

LIZ SONNEBORN

rosen central
Primary Source™

The Rosen Publishing Group, Inc., New York

Published in 2005 by The Rosen Publishing Group, Inc.
29 East 21st Street, New York, NY 10010

Copyright © 2005 by The Rosen Publishing Group, Inc.

First Edition

Library of Congress Cataloging-in-Publication Data

Sonneborn, Liz.
The Mexican-American War: a primary source history of the expansion of the western lands of the United States/by Liz Sonneborn.
    p. cm.—(Primary sources in American history)
Summary: Uses primary source documents, narrative, and illustrations to recount the history of the Mexican-American War.
Includes bibliographical references (p.) and index.
ISBN 1-4042-0180-7 (library binding)
1. Mexican War, 1846–1848—Juvenile literature. 2. Mexican War, 1846–1848—Juvenile literature. [1. Mexican War, 1846–1848. 2. Mexican War, 1846–1848–Sources.]
I. Title. II. Series: Primary sources in American history (New York, N.Y.)
E404.S68 2004
973.6'2—dc22

2003023341

Manufactured in the United States of America

On the front cover: *Genl. Taylor at the Battle of Palo Alto*, an 1846 lithograph by Currier and Ives.

On the back cover: First row (left to right): John Bakken's sod house in Milton, North Dakota; Oswego starch factory in Oswego, New York. Second row (left to right): *American Progress*, painted by John Gast in 1872; the Battle of Palo Alto. Third row (left to right): Pony Express rider pursued by Native Americans on the plains; Union soldiers investigating the rubble of a Southern building.

CONTENTS

NTRODUCTION

On April 25, 1846, a force of 1,600 Mexican soldiers came upon a small American scouting party near what is now Brownsville, Texas. Shots rang out. The Mexican-American War had begun.

Less than seventeen months later, the fighting was over. But the brief conflict had enormous consequences.

A WAR BETWEEN NEIGHBORS

With the war's end, one nation expanded its borders, taking in more than 500,000 square miles (1,295,000 sq kilometers) of new territory. The other was stripped of nearly half its land.

One nation emerged with a new sense of pride and confidence in its role as a world power. The other suffered the humiliation of watching its lands be invaded and occupied by a hated enemy.

One nation quickly relegated the war to history as its importance was overshadowed by later conflicts. The other continues to remember the war as a fresh wound that, after 150 years, has yet to heal.

For both nations, however, the Mexican-American War was a turning point. Because of the conflict, the way the United States and Mexico appeared to the world, to each other, and to themselves was forever changed.

TIMELINE

February 24, 1821	Mexico declares its independence from Spain.
April 21, 1836	Texas rebels defeat the Mexican army at San Jacinto.
November 5, 1844	James K. Polk is elected president after campaigning on an expansionist platform.
December 29, 1845	Texas officially enters the Union.
April 25, 1846	The American and Mexican armies exchange fire near what is now Brownsville, Texas.
May 8, 1846	American soldiers defeat the Mexican army in the Battle of Palo Alto.
May 13, 1846	U.S. Congress declares war on Mexico.
June 14, 1846	Bear Flag rebels declare California's independence from Mexico.
July 7, 1846	U.S. Navy seizes Monterey, California.

TIMELINE

September 21–23, 1846 — General Zachary Taylor's army takes the Mexican city of Monterrey.

February 22–23, 1847 — Taylor's troops defeat the Mexican army at Buena Vista.

March 9, 1847 — American forces led by General Winfield Scott land at Veracruz.

September 14, 1847 — American troops storm Mexico City.

February 2, 1848 — The Treaty of Guadalupe Hidalgo is signed.

May 30, 1848 — The Mexican Congress approves the Treaty of Guadalupe Hidalgo, officially ending the Mexican-American War.

CHAPTER 1

Before the war began, the countries of the United States and Mexico had been neighbors for twenty-five years. The relationship between these powers, however, was far from friendly. Years before the fighting began, each country had learned to be suspicious of the other. When Mexicans looked north, they saw a country of ruthless people, willing to do anything to increase their territory. When Americans looked south, they saw a nation of inferiors, unworthy of the rich lands they owned.

NATIONS IN CONFLICT

Two Young Nations

The festering hostility between the United States and Mexico had its roots in the early decades of the nineteenth century. As the century began, the United States was a young nation. Only seventeen years before, it had won its independence from British rule in the American Revolution (1775–1783). In that time, the country had prospered, largely by taking over land to the west of its original borders. Some of this territory was seized from Native American tribes, while other areas were purchased from European powers. The country's biggest land acquisition was the Louisiana Purchase of 1803, which brought its western border to the Rocky Mountains.

Created in 1844 and published for the U.S. State Department, this map shows Texas and the surrounding areas. At the time this map was drawn, Texas was an independent republic, no longer a province of Mexico, but considered valuable land by the United States. One year later, the United States would annex Texas, and the following year a war between the United States and Mexico would break out.

At the beginning of the nineteenth century, Mexico was not yet a country. Still called New Spain, its lands had been ruled by Spain for almost 300 years. But the native peoples of the region resented Spanish control and, in 1810, launched a long, bloody revolution. Finally, in 1821, the Spanish withdrew, and Mexico became an independent nation. Mexico took control of all Spanish-held territory in North America, including much of what is now the American West.

Mexico's troubles, however, were far from over. Once the Spanish were gone, the country had to create a new national government. But different political factions disagreed about how the country should be ruled. Also, several generals in the Mexican army wanted to take control over Mexico and rule as dictators. The fighting between these political and military leaders made the government highly unstable. Between 1821 and 1848, Mexico was ruled by more than twenty different administrations.

Amid this political chaos, Mexico was also facing an economic crisis. The country was deeply in debt. With most of its population concentrated in and around its capital, Mexico City, Mexico could not afford to protect outlying areas to the north. These largely unsettled lands were ripe for a foreign attack.

Settling Texas

Especially vulnerable was the Mexican province of Texas. Where river and streams flowed, the land in Texas was lush and fertile, perfect for farming. But few Mexicans wanted to venture this far north, especially since they knew their own government would provide little help or protection to settlers far from the capital. Land-hungry Americans were much more eager to make Texas their home. Thousands sneaked over the border and established homesteads on Mexican soil.

Unable to keep them out, the Mexican government decided to make American immigration work to its advantage. In 1824, it passed a law allowing Americans who pledged loyalty to Mexico to settle in Texas. Almost overnight, Texas was flooded with settlers, most from the American South.

Mexico assumed that the Texans would quickly become part of Mexican society. But most were far more interested in Mexican land than in Mexican ways. Living in isolated settlements, Texans had little contact with Mexicans. Many did not even bother to learn Spanish, the language of Mexico.

As more and more Americans arrived, the Mexican government worried that its plan had backfired. Instead of protecting them from invasion, American immigration was becoming an invasion, though one sanctioned by Mexican law. To stem the tide of new Texans, Mexico closed the border to Americans in 1830.

Revolt Against Mexico

The ban on American immigration infuriated the Texans. It prevented relatives back home from joining them and kept their settlements from growing. Texans also resented the Mexican government telling them what to do. Even though they were officially citizens of Mexico, at heart they thought of themselves as Americans.

Tensions reached a boiling point in June 1835. A small group of Texans decided to revolt. Mexico's president, Antonio López de Santa Anna, who was better known as Santa Anna, had little patience for the Texan rebels. He led thousands of soldiers

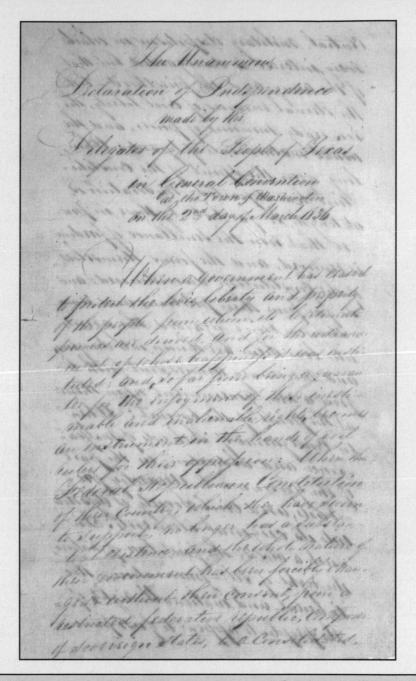

While the Alamo was under siege, representatives from each of the settlements of Texas formed the Convention of 1836. Five of the convention's delegates, George Childress, Edward Conrad, James Gaines, Bailey Hardeman, and Collin McKinney, drafted the Texas Declaration of Independence, shown above. Because of the need to act quickly, the declaration, which borrowed heavily from the United States' Declaration of Independence, was adopted only one day after its creation, on March 2, 1836. See transcription excerpt on page 57.

This portrait of Antonio López de Santa Ana (1794–1876), also known as Santa Anna, was painted by Paul L'Ouvrier around 1858. Santa Anna gained military fame in Mexico's fight against Spain, and his reputation as a hero in that war helped him become president of Mexico. Though he dominated Mexican politics for most of the nineteenth century, Santa Anna continually ignored what was best for his country. After a series of retirements and returns to lead Mexico, he died in his homeland, blind and impoverished.

north to crush the rebellion. At the Mexican post of San Antonio, Santa Anna's army met a force of about 150 Texans. Holed up in an abandoned mission called the Alamo, all the armed Texans were killed in the battle. Two weeks later, Santa Anna's men attacked the remaining Texan force at the fort at Goliad. After the Texans surrendered, a Mexican firing squad killed more than 300.

The brutality of Santa Anna only rallied more Texans to fight. Led by Sam Houston, new recruits waited for an opportunity to overtake the Mexican army. They got their chance when Santa Anna's men camped along the San Jacinto River in April 1836. While the Mexican soldiers were napping, Houston's force made a surprise attack. The Texans won the battle in twenty minutes. But for hours, they slaughtered hundreds of Mexican soldiers— a savage revenge for the Alamo and Goliad.

At San Jacinto, the Texans captured Santa Anna. He signed a treaty granting Texas independence from Mexico. The war was over, and the Republic of Texas was born.

The Republic of Texas

Back in Mexico City, Mexican leaders were furious at Santa Anna. They banished the president and refused to acknowledge the treaty he signed. As far as they were concerned, Mexico and Texas were still at war, even if Mexico did not have the troops available to continue the fight.

While the Texans considered themselves guardians of a new, independent country, many did not want to be. In September 1836, only months after the war's end, they voted for annexation— that is, to become part of the United States. But politicians in Washington were not so sure they wanted to annex Texas. The president, Andrew Jackson, worried it might start a war with Mexico. Many antislavery lawmakers also opposed the idea. Texas was largely settled by Southern slave owners, so it would likely enter the Union as a slave state.

The annexation debate continued, but it did not become a major issue until 1844. During that year's presidential election, Democratic candidate James K. Polk ran as an expansionist. He not only advocated annexing Texas but also wanted to expand

James K. Polk (1795-1849) worked tirelessly to attain the goals of his presidency: " . . . one, reduction of the tariff; another, an independent treasury; third, settlement of the Oregon boundary question; and lastly, the acquisition of California." The first two goals were achieved in 1846. He stood firm on the Oregon Territory boundary negotiations with Britain, avoiding an all-out war with the Oregon Compromise. And while his quest for the acquisition of California led to the Mexican-American War, he nevertheless achieved his goal.

America's western border all the way to the Pacific Coast. Polk's platform had enough popular appeal to win him the election.

Just before Polk took office, the U.S. Congress finally agreed to annex Texas. Caught up in expansionist fever, the wider American public cheered the annexation. To many Americans, it was a symbol of the great future their nation faced as it grew bigger and stronger. The people of Mexico, however, saw the annexation of Texas quite differently. To them, it was an act of war.

CHAPTER 2

In July 1845, the people of Texas voted to join the Union as the twenty-eighth state. Journalist John L. O'Sullivan celebrated the event in an article in the July–August 1845 issue of the journal *The United States Magazine and Democratic Review.* He declared that it was America's "manifest destiny to overspread the continent allotted by Providence for the free development of our yearly multiplying millions." With these words, O'Sullivan said it was the fate of the United States to take control of lands stretching across North America, from the Atlantic Ocean to the Pacific Ocean. What's more, O'Sullivan maintained that the nation's growth was "allotted by Providence," meaning that it was all part of God's plan. In the years to come, "manifest destiny" became a rallying cry for American expansionists.

ALONG THE RIO GRANDE

Diplomacy Fails

Among them was President Polk, who immediately after the Texas vote sent troops under General Zachary Taylor to the Nueces River. Although Mexico had never formally recognized Texas's independence, for almost ten years Mexicans had considered the river the informal boundary between Mexico and our power, limiting our greatness and checking the fulfilment of our manifest destiny to overspread the continent allotted by Providence for the free development of our yearly multiplying millions. This we have seen done by England, our old rival and enemy; and

This passage from the July and August 1845 issue of *The United States Magazine and Democratic Review* features the section on the Texas annexation written by John L. O'Sullivan in which he coined the term "manifest destiny." O'Sullivan cited England and France as nations whose example the United States should follow: "The zealous activity with which this effort to defeat us was pushed by the representatives of those governments . . . fully constituted that case of foreign interference, which . . . would unite us all in maintaining the common cause of our country against the foreigner and the foe."

Texas. Seeing American troops gathering along the Nueces infuriated the Mexican people. They saw the United States' actions as an insult to their national honor and wanted their government to take a stand.

The public's demands put enormous pressure on José Joaquín de Herrera, the new president of Mexico. To Herrera, the first priority was to improve his country's ailing economy. Fighting the American troops would only plunge the government deeper in debt. Herrera warned, "War with the United States over Texas is a bottomless abyss into which our Republic will sink along with all our hopes for the future."

Drawn from life by Captain Daniel Powers Whiting, this image shows a view of the camp of General Taylor's army near Corpus Christi, Texas. The army of occupation was the force used to accomplish the concept of manifest destiny. The army positioned itself by the Nueces River, which Mexico considered its northern boundary, in June 1845. President Polk had chosen occupation of this territory to provoke Mexico. The arrival of the army built up the small outpost of Corpus Christi, increasing the population from 100 to 2,000 and making the town's founder a rich man.

Herrera's best hope was negotiation. He agreed to talk with John Slidell, an American diplomat. Herrera believed if the United States was willing to pay Mexico for its loss of Texas, he might be able to squelch his people's thirst for war.

But before they could meet, Slidell's true mission was leaked to the Mexican press. Polk sent Slidell to offer up to $30 million for land in California and New Mexico. (New Mexico then included the present-day states of Arizona, Nevada, and Utah and portions of New Mexico, Wyoming, Colorado, and Oklahoma.) Both were valuable territories. California had lush farmland, and its coast featured several excellent ports. New Mexico included well-traveled

Mariano Paredes y Arrillaga (1797–1849), known as Don Mariano Paredes, is shown in the portrait on the left. Paredes initially supported Santa Anna, but later overthrew him. When Paredes became president of Mexico, he immediately led his country to war. He was brought down by Santa Anna and was unsuccessful in his future attempts to regain power. John Slidell (1793–1871), whose portrait is on the right, was an American congressman whom Polk sent to Mexico to negotiate with Mexican president Herrera.

trade routes, as well as Santa Fe, an important trading center where Mexicans, Americans, and Native Americans had long met to barter.

The United States' bid to take control over even more of Mexico further angered the Mexican people. To them, Herrera would be a traitor if he even considered the deal. Afraid of losing power, Herrera refused to see Slidell. Even so, Herrera's credibility was gone. Supported by a small group of wealthy Mexicans, General Mariano Paredes y Arrillaga marched an army into Mexico City and forced Herrera to resign. Naming himself the new president in January 1846, Paredes declared he would never surrender land to the Americans.

Armies Meet

Within a week of Paredes's inauguration, messengers informed Polk of Slidell's diplomatic failure. (At the time, it could take weeks for news to travel from Mexico City to Washington.) Polk decided to make his own stand. He sent word to General Taylor to march his army of 4,000 south to the Rio Grande.

It was a bold move. The American army was moving into a disputed area claimed by both countries. Polk, like many Americans, believed the Rio Grande marked the true border between Texas and Mexico. No Mexicans did, however. In their eyes, Taylor's men were clearly invading their country.

On March 28, 1846, the American army reached the Rio Grande, where they established Fort Texas (now Brownsville, Texas). Directly across the river was the Mexican military post of Matamoros. On April 25, 20 miles (32 km) from Fort Texas, Mexican soldiers encountered an American scouting party and opened fire. Fourteen Americans were killed. When Taylor found out about the conflict, he immediately wrote to the president, announcing that "hostilities may now be considered as commenced."

The Battle of Palo Alto

Two weeks later, the first battle of the war was fought. In early May, Taylor led most of his troops out of Fort Texas. They headed toward the Gulf of Mexico to meet ships carrying much-needed supplies. Along the way, at Palo Alto, they found the Mexican army waiting for them. More than 3,000 Mexican soldiers blocked the road in a line that stretched over a mile (1.6 km). Inflamed by the insulting presence of the American army, the soldiers were eager to fight. Flying brilliant banners high in the air, they shouted, "Viva la república!" (Long live the republic!), while a band playing patriotic songs further stirred their emotions.

The Battle of Palo Alto soon spelled disaster for the Mexicans. With inadequate financial support from the Mexican government, they were ill-equipped for battle. Facing an enemy that was both better trained and better armed, the Mexican soldiers were killed in huge numbers. In a letter to his wife, Napoleon Dana, a lieutenant in Taylor's army, wrote, "The battle was a horrid spectacle, corpses mangled most horribly."

After the Mexican defeat, the Americans crossed the Rio Grande, ready to take Matamoros by force. But with the Mexican army in retreat, the people of the town surrendered without firing a shot. The first battle of the war had allowed the American forces to push farther into Mexico and had left the Mexican army in shambles.

ferred so much of the report of the Secretary of War as relates to the Military Academy at West Point, made a report thereon, accompanied by a bill (No. 444) relating to the Military Academy at West Point: which bill was read a first and second time, and committed to the Committee of the Whole House on the state of the Union.

Mr. Thomasson gave notice of a motion for leave to introduce a bill to provide for the establishment of a post road from the District of Columbia to the Columbia river, in the Oregon Territory.

Mr. Brodhead, from the Committee on the Library, reported a resolution (No. 30) relative to an equestrian statue of Washington: which resolution was read a first and second time, and committed to the Committee of the Whole House on the state of the Union.

Mr. Gordon, from the select committee appointed on the 27th of March last upon the subject of the laws of the United States, and the purchase of a tenth volume of the same, made a report thereon, and recommend the adoption of the following resolution, viz:

Resolved, That the Clerk of this House cause to be distributed the tenth volume of the laws of the United States, in the same manner as the eighth and ninth volumes were distributed: which report and resolution were left upon the Speaker's table.

On motion of Mr. McKay, the House resolved itself into the Committee of the Whole House on the state of the Union; and, after some time spent therein, the Speaker resumed the chair, and Mr. Gordon reported that the committee having, according to order, had the state of the Union generally under consideration, particularly the bill (No. 116) making appropriations for the support of the Military Academy for the year ending on the 30th June, 1847, had come to no resolution thereon.

The following message was received from the President of the United States, by J. Knox Walker, his private secretary:

To the Senate and House of Representatives:

The existing state of the relations between the United States and Mexico renders it proper that I should bring the subject to the consideration of Congress. In my message at the commencement of your present session, the state of these relations, the causes which led to the suspension of diplomatic intercourse between the two countries in March, 1845, and the long-continued and unredressed wrongs and injuries committed by the Mexican government on citizens of the United States, in their persons and property, were briefly set forth.

As the facts and opinions which were then laid before you were carefully considered, I cannot better express my present convictions of the condition of affairs up to that time, than by referring you to that communication.

The strong desire to establish peace with Mexico on liberal and honorable terms, and the readiness of this government to regulate and adjust our boundary, and other causes of difference with that power, on such fair and equitable principles as would lead to permanent relations of the most friendly nature, induced me in September last to seek the reopening of diplomatic relations between the two countries. Every measure adopted on our part had for its object the furtherance of these desired results. In communicating to Congress a succinct statement of the injuries which we had suffered from Mexico, and which have been accumulating during

a period of more than twenty years, every expression that could tend to inflame the people of Mexico, or defeat or delay a pacific result, was carefully avoided. An envoy of the United States repaired to Mexico, with full powers to adjust every existing difference. But though present on the Mexican soil, by agreement between the two governments, invested with full powers, and bearing evidence of the most friendly dispositions, his mission has been unavailing. The Mexican government not only refused to receive him, or listen to his propositions, but, after a long-continued series of menaces, have at last invaded our territory, and shed the blood of our fellow-citizens on our own soil.

It now becomes my duty to state more in detail the origin, progress, and failure of that mission. In pursuance of the instructions given in September last, an inquiry was made, on the 13th of October, 1845, in the most friendly terms, through our consul in Mexico, of the minister for foreign affairs, whether the Mexican government "would receive an envoy from the United States intrusted with full powers to adjust all the questions in dispute between the two governments;" with the assurance that "should the answer be in the affirmative, such an envoy would be immediately despatched to Mexico." The Mexican minister, on the 15th of October, gave an affirmative answer to this inquiry, requesting, at the same time, that our naval force at Vera Cruz might be withdrawn, lest its continued presence might assume the appearance of menace and coercion pending the negotiations. This force was immediately withdrawn. On the 10th of November, 1845, Mr. John Slidell, of Louisiana, was commissioned by me as envoy extraordinary and minister plenipotentiary of the United States to Mexico, and was intrusted with full powers to adjust both the questions of the Texas boundary and of indemnification to our citizens. The redress of the wrongs of our citizens naturally and inseparably blended itself with the question of boundary. The settlement of the one question, in any correct view of the subject, involves that of the other. I could not, for a moment, entertain the idea that the claims of our much injured and long suffering citizens, many of which had existed for more than twenty years, should be postponed, or separated from the settlement of the boundary question.

Mr. Slidell arrived at Vera Cruz on the 30th of November, and was courteously received by the authorities of that city. But the government of General Herrera was then tottering to its fall. The revolutionary party had seized upon the Texas question to effect or hasten its overthrow. Its determination to restore friendly relations with the United States, and to receive our minister, to negotiate for the settlement of this question, was violently assailed, and was made the great theme of denunciation against it. The government of General Herrera, there is good reason to believe, was sincerely desirous to receive our minister; but it yielded to the storm raised by its enemies, and on the 21st of December refused to accredit Mr. Slidell upon the most frivolous pretexts. These are so fully and ably exposed in the note of Mr. Slidell, of the 24th of December last, to the Mexican minister of foreign relations, herewith transmitted, that I deem it unnecessary to enter into further detail on this portion of the subject.

Five days after the date of Mr. Slidell's note, General Herrera yielded the government to General Paredes, without a struggle, and on the 30th of December resigned the presidency. This revolution was accomplished solely by the army, the people having taken little part in the contest; and

50

This **May 11, 1846**, record from the *Journal of the House of Representatives* features President Polk's declaration of war with Mexico. Polk's original plan was to urge the country toward war, but he worried that he would be perceived as a bully. He was relieved to discover that fighting between the United States and Mexico had already broken out, although he could never have guessed the war would last as long as it did. See transcription excerpt on page 57.

Declaring War

While Mexicans and Americans were on the battlefield, Polk was meeting with his cabinet. Unaware that the fighting had already begun, the president was making a case for going to war against Mexico. Since his effort to buy California and New Mexico had failed, the only way to take over these valuable lands was to fight for them. But Polk knew he would have trouble getting support for war if the United States appeared to be the aggressor. On May 9, 1846, he tried to convince his cabinet ministers to support a preemptive strike against Mexico. As Polk recorded in his journal, "I stated that we had heard of no open act of aggression by the Mexican army, but that the danger was imminent."

Later that same evening, messengers from Mexico arrived in Washington. They delivered to Polk the note from General Taylor reporting the attack on the American scouting party two weeks earlier. It was welcome news to Polk. He no longer had to make a case for a preemptive strike. He could now argue that the war had already begun and that Mexico had started it.

Two days later, Polk appeared before the U.S. Congress. He declared, "After repeated menaces, Mexico has passed the boundary of the United States, and shed American blood upon the American soil." Obeying Polk's request, Congress passed a declaration of war against Mexico. At last, Polk had the war he had been hoping for.

CHAPTER 3

The formal declaration of war with Mexico set off an emotional debate in Washington. Most politicians supported the war, but a few still loudly opposed it. In the rest of the country, however, news of the war was celebrated. According to Carol and Thomas Christensen in their book *The U.S.–Mexican War* novelist Herman Melville described the excitement: "People . . . are all in a state of delirium about the Mexican War. A military ardor pervades all ranks . . . and apprentice boys are running off to the war by scores."

THE ARMIES OF THE WEST

Polk sent out a call for 50,000 volunteer soldiers, and the response was staggering. Young men from all over the country rushed to sign up to fight. In Polk's home state of Tennessee alone, almost 30,000 volunteers offered their services.

The Bear Flag Rebellion

As the military geared up, Polk developed a war strategy. He decided on a three-pronged approach. The navy would blockade Mexico's major ports to keep food and supplies from reaching its army. The fighting force led by General Taylor would fight on land, pushing into central Mexico. At the same time, a second

Above is the flag that was raised at the Bear Flag Rebellion. William Todd, a nephew of Mary Todd Lincoln's who had been raised in Abraham Lincoln's family, painted the design on a piece of unbleached cotton. The star was intended to reflect the lone star of Texas. The bear represented the great number of grizzlies in California. Although the original flag eventually burned in California's great earthquake and fire in 1906, its design influenced the state flag, which was adopted in 1911.

army would be sent west into New Mexico and California to secure these regions for the United States. Polk placed Colonel Stephen W. Kearny in charge of the Army of the West. On June 5, 1846, Kearny and 1,600 soldiers left Fort Leavenworth in what is now Kansas and began a long overland march toward Santa Fe.

While Kearny's army was heading out, violence broke out in California. At the time, Native Americans made up most of the California population. Only about 7,000 Mexicans lived in the province. A few hundred Americans had also settled in the Sacramento Valley of northern California. Most lived near Sutter's Fort, a trade center operated by a Swiss-German immigrant named John Sutter.

Despite their small numbers, the Americans in California made a daring bid for power. Led by explorer John Frémont, about 130 American men rebelled against Mexican rule in June 1846. For many years, the government in Mexico City had ignored California. With no military presence there, the Mexicans were largely at the mercy of this band of scruffy rebels.

The Americans rounded up several prominent Mexican landowners and imprisoned them in Sutter's Fort. Drunken on looted liquor, the Americans hoisted a flag painted with a crude picture of a grizzly bear on June 14. The Bear Flag rebels then declared themselves the leaders of the independent Republic of California.

The Navy Arrives

In early July 1846, Admiral John Drake Sloat led a squadron of ships into Monterey, a port in northern California. In the spring, Sloat had been sent to California by Polk with orders to take over the city of San Francisco if war broke out. Sloat had heard rumors of war, but once he found out about the Bear Flag Rebellion, he decided to act. Sloat raised the American flag over Monterey, then led a force overland to San Francisco. The Americans met no resistance. The Bear Flag rebels were happy to surrender their dubious hold on California to American troops. And, at least at first, the Mexicans were so relieved to be rid of the Bear Flaggers that they were willing to accept the authority of the U.S. Navy.

Sloat promised to restore peace to California. But he retired in late July, leaving Commodore Robert F. Stockton in command.

As the Bear Flag rebels were claiming California for themselves, U.S. Navy commander John D. Sloat was sailing to Monterey from Mexico on President Polk's orders. Sloat took possession of California from the rebels on July 7, 1846. The raising of the American flag over the Monterey presidio (military post) is depicted in this 1902 lithograph.

The aggressive Stockton was eager to make his name in battle. He took his men south, claiming the coastal towns of Santa Barbara and San Pedro for the United States.

Mexican officials tried to organize a force to fight the invaders, but with no funds to pay their soldiers, the desertion rate was high. Unable to muster a defense, the Mexicans of Los Angeles, the capital of California, watched silently as Stockton's army rode in and took control of the city on August 12.

Stephen Watts Kearny (1794–1848), whose portrait is shown on the left, excelled at using diplomacy rather than force in occupying western land for the United States. Kearny was able to accomplish many military victories and the establishment of a stable government in California, in spite of the obstacle of Robert Stockton (*right*), who refused to follow Kearny's lead. Stockton (1795–1866) captured Los Angeles and set up a civil government there. He later served in the U.S. Senate.

Taos Erupts

By mid-August, Kearny's army had established rule over New Mexico. Mexicans in the region had wanted to battle the troops. About 4,000 volunteers had been ready to fight, but their military commanders sent them home and then retreated, allowing the Americans to take Santa Fe without opposition.

The army's relationship with local Mexicans, however, remained tense. The Mexicans were especially resentful of Kearny's decision to make Charles Bent the province's governor in late September. Bent was an American trader, much despised by Mexicans for selling guns to their Native American enemies.

Leaving Bent in charge, Kearny took 300 troops and headed for California. The tensions between the Mexicans and Americans of New Mexico quickly grew worse. They reached the boiling point in January 1847, when a rebel force in the town of Taos murdered Bent and set American-owned businesses ablaze. American troops brutally squashed the rebellion. After killing about 150 Mexicans and Pueblo Indians, they arrested fifteen rebel leaders and, in a show trial, sentenced them to death.

The Battle for Los Angeles

As Taos burned, Kearny's men continued their hike toward Los Angeles. The trip was grueling. Day after day, they marched through the desert, often with very little food or water.

Messengers told Kearny that American troops had firm control over all of California. In fact, Mexicans repelled by Stockton's oppressive rule had decided to fight back. In Los Angeles, a force of 600 Mexicans had driven the American troops from the city.

New Mexico governor Charles Bent (1799–1847) was murdered in this room of his home in Taos, New Mexico, on January 19, 1847. Bent was a well-known trader, and his prominence in the area helped him win his position as governor, though it also led to the assassination of him and six other officials by Mexicans and Native Americans in the Taos revolt. The United States responded quickly and brutally, and punished the leaders of the revolt with public hangings.

Narrowly surviving their harrowing trip, Kearny's men walked into a war zone. On December 6, Kearny ordered a surprise attack on a Mexican force at the town of San Pascual. Although the Americans claimed victory at San Pascual, the battle took a toll on Kearny's men. In his 1848 book, *Notes of a Military Reconnaissance,* Lieutenant William H. Emory remembered that "their provisions were exhausted . . . their horses dead, their mules on their last legs; and the men, reduced by one-third their number, were ragged and worn."

Still, Kearny continued on to San Diego, where Stockton and his men had retreated. In early January, their combined forces headed north, overpowering the Mexican army in several hard-won battles along the way. On January 10, 1847, the Americans entered Los Angeles and reestablished rule over the city. With the soldiers' arrival, California had finally fallen into American hands.

CHAPTER 4

ON MEXICAN SOIL

As the American military struggled to gain control of California and New Mexico, General Zachary Taylor continued to push the war deeper into Mexico. Polk considered ordering Taylor's force to march all the way to Mexico City. The president wanted a quick end to the war and figured the easiest way to make Mexico surrender was to take its capital.

Taylor, however, discouraged the plan. His troops did not have nearly the supplies they needed for a 1,000-mile (1,609 km) march into unfamiliar territory. The general instead suggested a march on Monterrey, one of the largest cities in northern Mexico. Taylor insisted that if his troops secured the area, they could place enough pressure on the Mexican government to sue for peace.

To Monterrey

By the end of August 1846, about 6,600 American soldiers were under Taylor's command. That month, they set off on the month-long trek to Monterrey. As they approached, a Mexican force of 5,000 led by General Pedro de Ampudia prepared to mount an aggressive defense of the city. Anticipating a fierce battle, many of the people of Monterrey had fled. Families that could not

leave sent their children and elderly away to keep them out of harm's way.

The layout of the city presented the approaching American army with a challenge. The road leading into Monterrey took them by a high hill topped by a fortress called the Citadel. As the Americans tried to enter the city, Mexican cannon fire rained down on them. Thomas Thorpe, an American war correspondent, described the bombardment:

> The wind of passing balls and bombs continually fanned their faces . . . A twelve-pound shot literally passed through the closed ranks of the Tennessee regiment, throwing fragments of human beings into the air, and drenching the living with gore.

This Currier and Ives lithograph depicts the Battle of Monterrey, which took place from September 21 through September 23, 1846. Monterrey, Mexico, was an important fortress town that U.S. forces under Zachary Taylor tried to take. There was a three-day standoff between the two armies, until finally Taylor and Pedro de Ampudia signed an armistice that caused trouble on both sides. President Polk was furious with Taylor for negotiating a truce without having the authority, and Ampudia's actions demoralized his troops, setting the stage for Mexico's ultimate defeat.

On the second day of fighting, the Americans pushed into the city's center. From windows and rooftops, Mexican soldiers and civilians shot at the enemy. American soldiers went from house to house, bashing in doors to find the shooters. That night, Taylor's troops continued the battle, firing at Ampudia's headquarters, where the Mexicans had stored their ammunition. Fearing the

Thomas B. Thorpe (1815–1878) was an artist and humorist who wrote primarily about American frontier life. Thorpe reached the rank of colonel in the Mexican-American War and also served as a correspondent in that war. It is ironic that Thorpe would become known as a southwestern humorist, since he was born and raised in the Northeast, and indeed his ideals—including his position against slavery—were northern. Perhaps the greatest example of south-western humor was created by Thorpe, a piece called "The Big Bear of Arkansas," from *The Hive of The Bee-Hunter* (1854).

Americans would blow up their stronghold, Ampudia sent an aide to present the Americans with a white flag of surrender.

A Brief Peace

At first, Taylor demanded a complete surrender. But Ampudia proposed an armistice—a promise to stop the war temporarily. With his men too tired and hungry to fight anymore, Taylor agreed. The two armies pledged to suspend fighting for eight weeks, and Taylor allowed the Mexican force to keep their arms.

When President Polk heard about the armistice, he was furious. He thought Taylor had made a foolish mistake. In his diary, Polk wrote, "If General Taylor had captured the Mexican army and deprived them of their arms, it would have probably ended the war with Mexico."

Polk had another reason for being angry at Taylor. Now considered a war hero in the United States, Taylor was named as a possible candidate for the presidency. The general had become Polk's political rival, threatening his chance for reelection.

Polk sent off orders to Taylor. He told the general not to extend the armistice and to keep his troops in Monterrey. Taylor obeyed the first order but ignored the second. He moved his troops to the small town of Saltillo to ride out the armistice.

While occupying Saltillo, Taylor struggled to keep his troops under control. Despite his efforts, some young recruits committed acts of violence against Mexican civilians. Among the most horrible was the Rackensacker Massacre. The Rackensackers were an especially wild group of volunteers from Arkansas. After Mexicans killed a soldier for insulting a Mexican woman, the Rackensackers took a bloody revenge. They rounded up some twenty Mexicans and slaughtered them.

Santa Anna Returns

In the meantime, the Mexican army regrouped at its new headquarters at San Luis Potosí. They were now led by Santa Anna, the former president of Mexico who had been driven out of office after the Texas Revolution. Since then, two Mexican presidents—José Joaquín de Herrera and Mariano Paredes y Arrillaga—had been overthrown. The regime of the current president, General Mariano Salas, also seemed in danger since Santa Anna had returned to Mexico in August. Despite his past military mistakes, many Mexicans thought only Santa Anna could lead them to victory.

Santa Anna was certainly successful at recruiting new soldiers. Largely because of his charismatic personality, he was able to assemble an army of 20,000 at San Luis Potosí. He had far more difficulty convincing the government in Mexico City to fund his growing army. After Monterrey fell, President Salas tried to raise property taxes to finance the war, but the Mexican people began rioting before the taxes were even collected. The government's inability to send needed money and supplies soon poisoned the soldiers' morale. In his autobiography, *The Eagle,* Santa Anna recalled, "The soldiers grew more anxious with each passing day. 'No one wants to send even bread and meat to the army,' they grumbled."

President Salas's further attempts to raise money proved his undoing. When he tried to levy taxes on the wealthy and the clergy, these powerful forces overthrew him. In December 1846, Santa Anna once again became the president of Mexico.

Scott Takes Charge

As the armistice drew to a close, Polk changed his war strategy. He had lost all confidence in Taylor. According to Carol and Thomas Christensen, the president wrote in his diary, "General Taylor is very hostile to the administration . . . I am now convinced that he is a narrow-minded, bigoted partisan . . . wholly unqualified for the position he now holds."

Polk decided to place military command of the Mexican war front in the hands of General Winfield Scott. Scott would bring fresh troops by sea to the Mexican coastal town of Veracruz. There, he would also take charge of about half of Taylor's force and continue overland to Mexico City.

When Taylor got word of the new plan, he was appalled. Many of his men were also upset that the general was effectively being relieved of his command. According to the Christensens,

Lieutenant Napoleon Dana, who had followed Taylor into Monterrey, wrote to his wife:

> We believe him the greatest general our country had produced, and there is nothing the army will not do for that old chief . . . It is useless for such insignificant pygmies as J. K. Polk to beat their brains out against such men as he.

The Battle of Buena Vista

At San Luis Potosí, Santa Anna felt increasing pressure to attack. Mexicans were calling him a coward because he had not led his large army into battle. When Santa Anna learned that half of Taylor's army had left for Veracruz, he saw a chance to restore the public's confidence in him. Even though his supplies were dangerously low, he ordered his 20,000-man army to march toward Saltillo on January 27, 1847.

The 240-mile (386 km) trek was agonizing. Camping in freezing temperatures, some soldiers died of exposure. Others gave up on the mission and deserted. In just a few weeks, Santa Anna's army was down to 15,000 soldiers. Santa Anna also had bad news from Mexico City. His vice president had tried to raise money by auctioning off church property, leading the clergy to threaten to overthrow Santa Anna's new presidency.

Scouts told Taylor of the Mexicans' approach. He moved his army to Buena Vista, 5 miles (8 km) south of Saltillo, and waited. On February 22, the Americans spied the Mexican army on the horizon. That day and the next, the two armies fought fiercely. As the Christensens quote, General Andrés Terrés y Masaguér of the Mexican army recalled, "The combat was bloody; both armies moved as close as the terrain would allow and fought

Created circa 1847, this map shows a bird's-eye view of the Battle of Buena Vista, which took place on February 22 and 23, 1847. Zachary Taylor had moved his troops to Buena Vista, a pass between two mountain ranges. When Santa Anna's troops arrived, the fighting that ensued was fierce and bloody. The estimated casualties were 1,500 of Santa Anna's troops and 700 of Taylor's troops.

with desperate courage." Although outnumbered, the Americans managed to hold their position.

On the third day, the American army woke up to a surprise. Santa Anna's men were gone. They had retreated in the dark of night. Many Mexicans were outraged when they heard the news. They believed Santa Anna would have surely won this pivotal battle if only he had chosen to stay and fight. Years later, in his autobiography, Santa Anna claimed he had retreated because the Mexican government demanded his troops return to Mexico City to protect the capital. Another explanation he gave soon after the battle was possibly closer to the truth. Left without food or water for two days, his soldiers were simply too exhausted to fight.

CHAPTER 5

While Santa Anna and Taylor battled at Buena Vista, Scott was amassing his army just off the Mexican coast on the Isle of Lobos. By early March 1847, he had about 12,000 soldiers under his command with more volunteers on the way. Scott carefully planned his next step: landing his troops on the shore at the town of Veracruz. From Veracruz, they could march down Mexico's National Road, which led directly to Mexico City.

The Attack on Veracruz

THE FIGHT FOR MEXICO CITY

When Scott was ready, he alerted General Juan Morales, the commander in charge of the fort at Veracruz. The American general gave Morales a chance to surrender. Scott guaranteed that the town's civilians would not be harmed if Morales agreed to his terms. Although there were only 1,600 soldiers at the fort, Morales refused.

Scott then began his siege on the city. His troops surrounded the stone walls around the city, cutting off all Mexican supply routes. After intensive shelling, the Americans blew through the walls, leaving the population of Veracruz at their mercy. According to the Christensens, Robert E. Lee, who

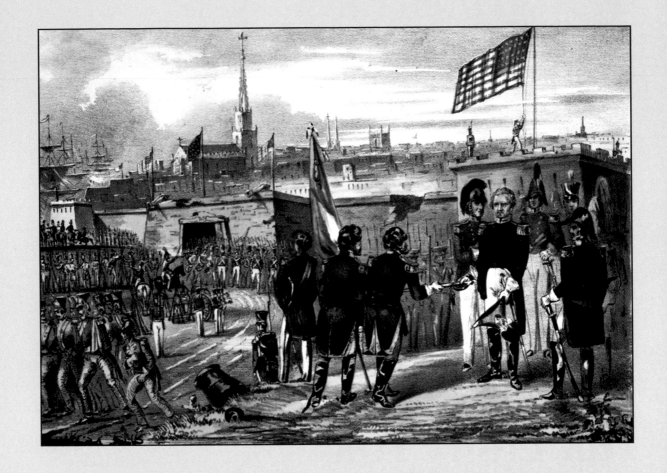

As commanding general of the U.S. Army, Winfield Scott (1786–1866) recommended Zachary Taylor to command U.S. forces in the Mexican-American War. But Scott was disgusted with Taylor for failing to follow Santa Anna's troops farther into Mexico after the Battle of Buena Vista. Scott took over the operation, sailing to Veracruz himself. After a three-week siege, Scott took Veracruz, then began a march into Mexico City.

served as a captain in Scott's army, wrote in a letter home, "It was awful! My heart bled for the inhabitants. The soldiers I did not care so much for, but it was terrible to think of the women and children." Morales resigned, and his successor surrendered the city to the American force.

The Polkos Revolt

By the time Veracruz fell, Santa Anna had rushed back to Mexico City. There, he faced a new battle, but the enemy was not American. It was a group of upper-class soldiers that were rebelling against the Mexican government. The rebels were outraged by the vice president's attempt to sell church property to fund the war effort. Critics of the rebels snidely called the uprising the Polkos Revolt after a dance then popular among wealthy Mexicans.

Sizing up the situation, Santa Anna cleverly negotiated an agreement with the Mexican clergy. He agreed to let them keep their property. In return, they promised to give him $2 million for his troops.

Santa Anna had saved his position and put down the rebellion. But he still had to deal with Scott's army. About a week after the surrender of Veracruz, the American force began moving along the National Road toward the Mexican capital. With no time to lose, Santa Anna reassembled his army and led it to Cerro Gordo, a large hill about 50 miles (80 km) inland from Veracruz. There, Santa Anna's soldiers mounted guns and waited for the Americans to arrive.

Cerro Gordo

Scott suspected that Santa Anna would try to block his troops' advance, but he did not know where. To find out, he sent out a scouting mission led by Captain Robert E. Lee and Lieutenant Pierre G.T. Beauregard, men who would later be important players in the Civil War. Based on their reports, Scott decided to circle around Cerro Gordo, thus avoiding the head-on encounter Santa Anna was expecting.

On April 18, the battle between the two forces began. The Americans fought hard, driving many Mexican soldiers to flee. Those that could not were soon surrounded. As the Mexicans surrendered, Santa Anna managed to escape. Many of his men were not so lucky. More than 3,000 were taken prisoner.

The quick defeat was humiliating to the Mexican army. Scott fully expected the enemy to give up, but Santa Anna was determined to keep fighting. He brought what was left of his army back to Mexico City.

At Puebla

Scott and his men soon continued down the National Road. They stopped their advance at Puebla, about 100 miles (161 km) from the Mexican capital. There, Scott's men settled in. They occupied the city for three months, as the general waited for reinforcements.

The Americans met no resistance as they entered Puebla, which was then the second largest city in Mexico. The citizens of Puebla, however, were far from happy about their presence. They found the American soldiers crude and undisciplined. A Mexican journalist wrote in the newspaper *Diario* that the American army was "made up of adventurers who have no . . . religious creed, no moral principles or sentiments."

Some Americans also began to wonder how disciplined Scott and his soldiers were. They were growing impatient as

In April 1847, General Scott moved his weary army of 8,500 men westward to Plan del Rio, near Cerro Gordo, where they met an overpowering force of 12,000 of Santa Anna's men. Thanks to the efforts of American engineering forces, including future Confederate general Robert E. Lee, a hidden path was discovered and Scott was able to get around the Mexican army. Santa Anna fled to Mexico City, as depicted in this lithograph, leaving thousands of dead and imprisoned troops behind.

Scott waited for the most advantageous time to attack. The American public compared the deliberate and careful Scott unfavorably to Taylor, who was far more willing to take risks, even if they put his men in greater danger.

Negotiations Begin

President Polk was also losing confidence in Scott. Reports from the front persuaded him that it was perhaps time to negotiate. He sent Nicholas Trist, a diplomat fluent in Spanish, to Mexico with a sealed letter in hand on April 15, 1847. In the letter, Polk said he would accept a Mexican surrender only if Santa Anna gave up Texas, New Mexico, and California. In exchange, Trist was authorized to offer the Mexican government up to $30 million.

In July, Trist convinced Santa Anna to meet with him. But, by that time, the Mexican Congress had passed a law making it illegal to negotiate with the United States. If Santa Anna accepted Trist's terms, he would be committing treason.

But, in fact, Santa Anna was only pretending to negotiate. He made demands he knew Trist would not agree to. All the while, Santa Anna was buying time, preparing his troops for their last stand against the Americans.

Valencia's Battle

On August 7, Scott's army reached the edge of the Valley of Mexico. In the center of this great valley was Mexico City. Surrounded by swampland, there were only a few roads in and out of the city, making it relatively easy to defend. Santa Anna assembled the bulk of his forces on a hill overlooking the main road.

With the help of scouts, Scott plotted a way into the city that would bypass these troops. He decided to circle around and attack the city from the south. As his army began marching, the citizens of Mexico City fled from their homes, no longer confident their soldiers could protect them.

As Scott approached the town of Contreras, he was surprised by a Mexican force of 7,000 troops led by General Gabriel Valencia. Santa Anna had ordered all troops to stay close to Mexico City, but Valencia, a longtime rival of Santa Anna's, defied the commander. After a day of fighting, Santa Anna demanded Valencia retreat, but he refused. As the Mexican leaders squabbled, Scott's

Nicholas Trist (1800–1874) was serving as chief clerk in the State Department when President Polk assigned him to negotiate a peace treaty with Santa Anna. By this time, Polk had lost confidence in yet another of his men—this time it was Winfield Scott. Because of delays with the Mexican government, which was really Santa Anna's crafty way of buying time to get his troops in order, Trist had no choice but to wait to begin his negotiations. Polk became impatient with Trist and ordered him to return to Washington.

troops repositioned themselves during the night. Surrounding Valencia's troops, the Americans attacked in the morning and forced a surrender in only seventeen minutes. Many Mexican soldiers fled north to Churubusco, where the fighting continued. In the bloody battle there, casualties were high on both sides.

The Final Fight

Valencia's miscalculation left the Mexican army in shambles. Scott could probably have defeated Santa Anna, but instead he stopped his pursuit. Scott believed the Mexicans were now truly ready to talk peace.

Scott proposed an armistice, and Santa Anna agreed. But again the Mexican leader had no real interest in negotiating. He instead spent the brief peace fortifying Mexico City. In a proclamation to the city's residents, he declared, "The enemy lifts the sword to strike your front ranks; we too will raise it to punish the rancorous pride of the invader."

Soon, Scott had had enough of Santa Anna's stalling. On September 7, he returned to the battlefield. Scott first ordered his troops to take over a mill at Molino Del Rey, where he was told Mexicans were making cannonballs. The battle was a bloodbath. Scott lost many troops before learning that his intelligence reports about the site were wrong.

His men continued on to the Castle of Chapultepec, which then housed the Mexican military academy. High on a hill, the fortress was heavily guarded by Mexican troops. American soldiers stormed the building, using ladders to scale its high walls. After hours of hand-to-hand combat, the Americans took Chapultepec.

Among the Mexican defenders of the Castle of Chapultepec was a group of cadets studying at Mexico's military academy. Six

This Mexico City monument is dedicated to Los Niños Héroes, six teenagers who fought along with 5,000 other Mexicans in the Battle at Chapultepec, the last obstacle Winfield Scott faced on his way to Mexico City. The boys were studying at Mexico's military academy, and they fought valiantly to defend the Castle of Chapultepec, choosing to die rather than surrender to U.S. forces. Some accounts hold that one cadet wrapped himself in the Mexican flag before leaping from the castle walls to his death.

cadets chose to die rather than surrender. Known as Los Niños Héroes ("the heroic children"), they are still honored in Mexico each year with a national memorial ceremony.

After the battle at Chapultepec, the troops then headed on to Mexico City itself. After battling through soldiers guarding a roadway, they met fire from Mexican citizens, stationed on rooftops, determined to protect their homes. The battle stopped as night fell. In the darkness, Santa Anna met with his generals and staff. Before dawn, the Mexican leader boarded a carriage and fled, leaving the capital in the hands of the enemy.

CHAPTER 6

At four in the morning on September 14, 1847, a group of Mexican leaders arrived at General Winfield Scott's headquarters. Santa Anna had disappeared, leaving the Mexican army without a commander. The city leaders realized they had no choice but to surrender the capital to the invading American force.

With Scott's army in control of Mexico City, the Mexican government moved to the town of Querétaro. There, Manuel de la Peña y Peña took over as the acting president. Peña y Peña was eager to work out a treaty with diplomat Nicholas Trist. The Mexican president feared his country might not survive further hostilities with the United States.

DEFEAT AND VICTORY

The Treaty of Guadalupe Hidalgo

Nicholas Trist was preparing for the treaty negotiations when he received a disturbing letter from Secretary of State James Buchanan. It ordered Trist to return home immediately. Dated October 6, 1847, the letter said President Polk now believed that Trist's "continued presence with the army can be productive of no good, but may do harm by encouraging the delusive hopes and false impressions of the Mexicans."

The Treaty of Guadalupe Hidalgo was signed on February 2, 1848, and brought an official end to the Mexican-American War. Defying President Polk, Nicholas Trist went ahead and negotiated the treaty with Mexico. For the United States, Trist acquired northern California and New Mexico (these territories include present-day Arizona and New Mexico and parts of Utah, Nevada, and Colorado) in exchange for $15 million compensation for war damage. See transcription excerpt on pages 57–58.

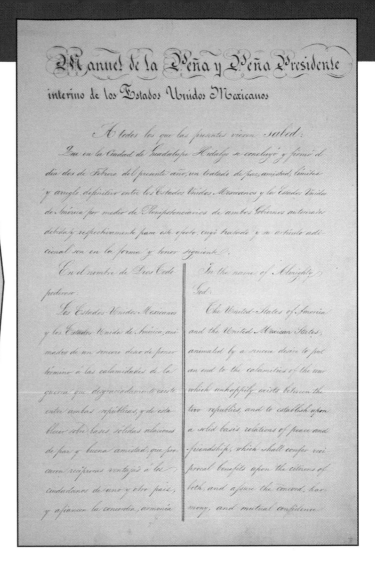

Polk had learned that during the brief armistice in August, Trist had discussed setting the border of Texas at the Nueces River rather than at the Rio Grande. The news annoyed Polk. He rashly decided that the Mexicans, not Trist, should initiate the peace process.

Trist was stunned. Both he and Peña y Peña were convinced that opening negotiations as soon as possible was crucial to establishing a lasting peace. Trist decided to continue his mission, even if it meant defying the president of the United States. He wrote a letter to Polk, explaining that if the "opportunity [to negotiate] be not seized at once, all chance of making a treaty at all will be lost . . . probably forever."

By the end of January, Trist and three Mexican negotiators had hashed out a treaty. It called for Mexico to surrender Texas, New Mexico, and nearly all of California. Only the peninsula of Baja California would remain part of Mexico. In exchange, the United States pledged to give Mexico $15 million. On February 2, 1848, the negotiators on both sides met at the town of Guadalupe Hidalgo and signed the agreement.

Debating the Treaty

About two weeks later, the treaty arrived in Washington. Polk was still angry at Trist, but he was pleased with the terms of the treaty. He sent it on to the Senate for ratification.

The treaty sparked a hot debate. Some senators felt the United States was settling for too little. They thought America should seize all of Mexico. Others felt it was grabbing too much. They believed the invasion of Mexico had been unwarranted and immoral. The treaty terms also reignited the concerns of the antislavery faction. They were hesitant about annexing any Mexican territory, for fear it would be organized into slave states. In the end, however, the Senate voted to ratify the treaty on March 10.

In Mexico, the Treaty of Guadalupe Hidalgo also inspired a spirited discussion. Some Mexicans did not want the war to end. They could not accept the idea of losing so much territory after so much blood had been spilled to protect it. But Peña y Peña urged his citizens to put their grief and pride aside and end the war for the good of future generations. He proclaimed, "Let us do the right thing, gentlemen. Let us strip off the veil that has prevented us from seeing the reality of things. Let us make a mighty effort, so that our children will not curse our memory." On May 30, the Mexican Congress approved the treaty, marking the official end of the Mexican-American War.

Winners and Losers

For Polk, the treaty was a personal victory. Going to war with Mexico was a big gamble, and he had won. He had made good on his campaign promise to bring Texas, New Mexico, and California into the Union. Polk's luck, however, soon ran out. Due to bad health, he decided not to run for a second term. Polk returned home to Tennessee, where he died three months later.

Celebrated as a war hero, Zachary Taylor was elected to the presidency in 1848, signaling a transfer of power from the Democratic Party to the Whig Party. Taylor died of cholera two years later, allowing another war veteran, General Winfield Scott, to secure the Whig nomination in 1852. Scott, however, lost his presidential bid to Franklin Pierce, who had served under him during the war.

In Mexico, Santa Anna left his country in disgrace, fleeing to the island of Jamaica. After just four years, however, he briefly returned to power. Before being once again overthrown, he brought $10 million into Mexico's treasury through the Gadsden Purchase—the sale to the United States of a small strip of land in what are now southern Arizona and southern New Mexico.

Postwar Mexico

In general, for Mexico, the war had been devastating. The government was bankrupt. Many important buildings and roads were destroyed. Thousands of Mexicans—both soldiers and civilians—were dead or wounded. And the size of the country had been cut in half.

But perhaps worst of all was the psychological blow to the Mexican people. They had been humiliated by invasion and occupation by a foreign people. The shock and sorrow at war's end, however, made the Mexican people take a good look at their country and their government. Their leaders began to make overdue reforms in their political and social structure. In the decades to come, Mexicans voted for moderate leaders who helped bring relief to the country's poorest citizens. The leaders also worked to limit the overwhelming power of Mexico's clergy and military.

In addition, the war helped shape a new national identity for Mexico. It was clear that the Mexican people had been partly to blame for the American victory, since warring factions in their government and their society were unable to come together in this time of crisis. After sharing the trauma of invasion, Mexicans were much more willing to put their differences aside for the good of their country.

Conquered People

The aftermath of the war was equally jarring for the people who lived in the lands ceded to the United States. Under Mexican rule, the Native Americans of California and the Southwest remained independent. They occasionally skirmished with Mexican settlers when they felt their land and its resources were threatened. But, without the manpower available to police these northern provinces, the Mexican government largely left these Native Americans alone.

Almost immediately after the war, however, the American presence became overwhelming in these regions. In January 1848, even before the Treaty of Guadalupe Hidalgo was signed, gold was discovered at Sutter's Fort in California. Over the next decade, miners from the eastern United States flooded into the area. In California, many Native Americans were killed or enslaved. Between 1850 and 1860, the Native American population of California was reduced by two-thirds.

In other areas ceded by Mexico, Indian groups were set upon by the U.S. military in the late nineteenth century. In order to seize their lands for white settlement, the United States warred with the Navajos, Comanches, Apaches, Kiowas, and other smaller groups. Over time, these peoples were stripped of much of their territory and forced to live on reservations, where retaining their traditional ways was often all but impossible.

Native Americans were greatly affected by the land allocations mandated by the Treaty of Guadalupe Hidalgo. During the U.S. military's attempt to defeat Native American tribes, a tragedy known as the Kidder Massacre occurred, presumably at the hands of angry Cheyenne and Sioux peoples. En route to relay a dispatch to George Custer, Lieutenant Lyman S. Kidder and his troops were mutilated, burned, and scalped at Fort Sedgewick, near Jelesburg, Colorado. The illustration above shows Custer arriving with his soldiers to the site of the Kidder Massacre.

The transfer of western lands from Mexico to the United States also had a devastating effect on the 75,000 Mexicans living in this area. By the terms of the Treaty of Guadalupe Hidalgo, these people could elect to stay or return to Mexico. Most stayed, but the legal and property rights guaranteed to them were soon eroded. Treated like second-class citizens, the Mexicans saw their land and wealth confiscated as more Americans moved into this newly acquired territory.

A New America

The United States was also transformed by the outcome of the Mexican-American War. Most obviously, the country became much larger, acquiring more than 500,000 square miles (1,295,000 sq kilometers) of territory. Hundreds of thousands of Americans moved west to seek their fortune—some by building homesteads on inexpensive farmland, others by taking advantage of the region's rich natural resources. Gaining control over California's port cities was an additional boon to America, allowing it to pursue lucrative trade with Asia.

Yet, in some ways, the United States paid a heavy price for its victory. The American military had lost many soldiers in the war. Bringing so much new territory into the country also stirred up the emotions of the nation's pro-slavery and antislavery factions. The Mexican-American War, therefore, helped inflame the tensions that only thirteen years later erupted into the American Civil War (1861–1865)—a horrific conflict that nearly destroyed the country.

The addition of western territories led to other bloody conflicts with the Indian and Hispanic populations of the region. It also increased racial prejudice in American culture. For many Americans, the defeat of Mexico was proof of the superiority of Anglo-Americans. The war therefore helped bolster racist beliefs and provided a model for using racism to justify aggression against foreign peoples.

The war also compromised the way Americans liked to view themselves. Since the American Revolution, the United States was celebrated as a land of liberty and justice, a place where all people would be treated fairly. While most Americans accepted that Mexico had started the Mexican-American War, some questioned this claim. In their eyes, the United States was the aggressor, choosing to invade a weaker country in order to seize its land. Among these Americans was Nicholas Trist, the diplomat who negotiated

Published in 1847, this map of Mexico was used for negotiations in the Treaty of Guadalupe Hidalgo and is referenced in Article V of the treaty. A copy of the map, which was a revised edition published in New York by John Disturnell, was attached to the document for use as a resource in illustrating the boundaries drawn by the treaty. The treaty stated, "The boundary lines established by this article shall be religiously respected by each of the two republics, and no change shall ever be made therein, except by the express and free consent of both nations."

the treaty that ended the war. While signing the treaty, one Mexican negotiator spoke of his humiliation at his country's defeat. Trist later recalled, "Could those Mexicans have seen into my heart at that moment, they would have known that my feeling of shame as an American was far stronger than theirs could be."

PRIMARY SOURCE TRANSCRIPTIONS

Page 11 Texas Declaration of Independence

Transcription excerpt

The Unanimous Declaration of Independence Made by the Delegates of the People of Texas in General Convention at the Town of Washington on the 2nd day of March 1836.

These, and other grievances, were patiently borne by the people of Texas, untill they reached that point at which forbearance ceases to be a virtue. We then took up arms in defence of the national constitution. We appealed to our Mexican brethren for assistance. Our appeal has been made in vain. Though months have elapsed, no sympathetic response has yet been heard from the Interior. We are, therefore, forced to the melancholy conclusion, that the Mexican people have acquiesced in the destruction of their liberty, and the substitution therfor of a military government; that they are unfit to be free, and incapable of self government. The necessity of self-preservation, therefore, now decrees our eternal political separation.

We, therefore, the delegates with plenary powers of the people of Texas, in solemn convention assembled, appealing to a candid world for the necessities of our condition, do hereby resolve and declare, that our political connection with the Mexican nation has forever ended, and that the people of Texas do now constitute a free, Sovereign, and independent republic, and are fully invested with all the rights and attributes which properly belong to independent nations; and, conscious of the rectitude of our intentions, we fearlessly and confidently commit the issue to the decision of the Supreme arbiter of the destinies of nations.

Page 21 Polk's Declaration of War

Transcription excerpt

The strong desire to establish peace with Mexico on liberal and honorable terms, and the readiness of this government to regulate and adjust our boundary, and other causes of difference with that power, on such fair and equitable principles as would lead to permanent relations of the most friendly nature, induced me in September last to seek the reopening of diplomatic relations between the two countries. Every measure adopted on our part had for its object the furtherance of these desired results. In communicating to Congress a succinct statement of the injuries which we had suffered from Mexico, and which have been accumulating during a period of more than twenty years, every expression that could tend to inflame the people of Mexico, or defeat or delay a pacific result, was carefully avoided. An envoy of the United States repaired to Mexico, with full powers to adjust every existing difference. But though present on the Mexican soil, by agreement between the two governments, invested with full powers, and bearing evidence of the most friendly dispositions, his mission has been unavailing. The Mexican government not only refused to receive him, or listen to his propositions, but, after a long-continued series of menaces, have at last invaded our territory, and shed the blood of our fellow-citizens on our own soil.

Page 49 Treaty of Guadalupe Hidalgo

Transcription excerpt

TREATY OF PEACE, FRIENDSHIP, LIMITS, AND SETTLEMENT BETWEEN THE UNITED STATES OF AMERICA AND THE UNITED MEXICAN STATES CONCLUDED AT GUADALUPE HIDALGO, FEBRUARY 2, 1848; RATIFICATION ADVISED BY SENATE, WITH AMENDMENTS, MARCH 10, 1848; RATIFIED BY PRESIDENT, MARCH 16, 1848; RATIFICATIONS EXCHANGED AT QUERETARO, MAY 30, 1848; PROCLAIMED, JULY 4, 1848. IN THE NAME OF ALMIGHTY GOD

The United States of America and the United Mexican States animated by a sincere desire to put an end to the calamities of the war which unhappily exists between the two Republics and to establish Upon a solid basis relations of peace and friendship, which shall confer reciprocal benefits upon the citizens of both, and assure the concord, harmony, and mutual confidence wherein the two people should live, as good neighbors have for that purpose appointed their respective plenipotentiaries, Who, after a reciprocal communication of their respective full powers, have, under the protection of Almighty God, the author of peace, arranged, agreed upon, and signed the following: Treaty of Peace, Friendship, Limits, and Settlement between the United States of America and the Mexican Republic.

ARTICLE I

There shall be firm and universal peace between the United States of America and the Mexican Republic, and between their respective countries, territories, cities, towns, and people, without exception of places or persons.

The southern and western limits of New Mexico, mentioned in the article, are those laid down in the map entitled "Map of the United Mexican States, as organized and defined by various acts of the Congress of said republic, and constructed according to the best authorities. Revised edition. Published at New York, in 1847, by J. Disturnell," of which map a copy is added to this treaty, bearing the signatures and seals of the undersigned Plenipotentiaries. And, in order to preclude all difficulty in tracing upon the ground the limit separating Upper from Lower California, it is agreed that the said limit shall consist of a straight line drawn from the middle of the Rio Gila, where it unites with the Colorado, to a point on the coast of the Pacific Ocean, distant one marine league due south of the southernmost point of the port of San Diego, according to the plan of said port made in the year 1782 by Don Juan Pantoja, second sailing-master of the Spanish fleet, and published at Madrid in the year 1802, in the atlas to the voyage of the schooners Sutil and Mexicana; of which plan a copy is hereunto added, signed and sealed by the respective Plenipotentiaries. The boundary line established by this article shall be religiously respected by each of the two republics, and no change shall ever be made therein, except by the express and free consent of both nations, lawfully given by the General Government of each, in conformity with its own constitution.

ARTICLE VIII

Mexicans now established in territories previously belonging to Mexico, and which remain for the future within the limits of the United States, as defined by the present treaty, shall be free to continue where they now reside, or to remove at any time to the Mexican Republic, retaining the property which they possess in the said territories, or disposing thereof, and removing the proceeds wherever they please, without their being subjected, on this account, to any contribution, tax, or charge whatever.

Those who shall prefer to remain in the said territories may either retain the title and rights of Mexican citizens, or acquire those of citizens of the United States. But they shall be under the obligation to make their election within one year from the date of the exchange of ratifications of this treaty; and those who shall remain in the said territories after the expiration of that year, without having declared their intention to retain the character of Mexicans, shall be considered to have elected to become citizens of the United States.

ARTICLE IX

The Mexicans who, in the territories aforesaid, shall not preserve the character of citizens of the Mexican Republic, conformably with what is stipulated in the preceding article, shall be incorporated into the Union of the United States and be admitted at the proper time (to be judged of by the Congress of the United States) to the enjoyment of all the rights of citizens of the United States, according to the principles of the Constitution; and in the mean time, shall be maintained and protected in the free enjoyment of their liberty and property, and secured in the free exercise of their religion without restriction.

ARTICLE XI

Considering that a great part of the territories, which, by the present treaty, are to be comprehended for the future within the limits of the United States, is now occupied by savage tribes, who will hereafter be under the exclusive control of the Government of the United States, and whose incursions within the territory of Mexico would be prejudicial in the extreme, it is solemnly agreed that all such incursions shall be forcibly restrained by the Government of the United States whensoever this may be necessary; and that when they cannot be prevented, they shall be punished by the said Government, and satisfaction for the same shall be exacted all in the same way, and with equal diligence and energy, as if the same incursions were meditated or committed within its own territory, against its own citizens.

ARTICLE XII

In consideration of the extension acquired by the boundaries of the United States, as defined in the fifth article of the present treaty, the Government of the United States engages to pay to that of the Mexican Republic the sum of fifteen millions of dollars.

GLOSSARY

annex To make an area part of an existing country or state.

armistice A temporary end to fighting agreed on by warring enemies.

clergy People ordained for religious service.

dictator A ruler with complete authority.

expansionism The policy of trying to expand a nation's territory.

fortify To prepare to protect an area from enemy attack.

immigration Movement to a new country with the intent of permanently settling there.

manifest destiny The idea that the United States was fated to expand from the Atlantic Ocean to the Pacific Ocean.

preemptive Relating to a military attack made before an expected strike by an enemy.

providence The control of a supreme being over life on Earth.

ratify To formally approve a treaty.

siege The surrounding of a city or fort by an army in an attempt to capture it.

treason The crime of betraying one's country.

FOR MORE INFORMATION

Palo Alto Battlefield National Historic Site
1623 Central Boulevard, Room 213
Brownsville, TX 78520-2785
(956) 541-2785
Web site: http://www.nps.gov/paal

Santa Fe National Historic Trail
National Trails System Office—Santa Fe
P.O. Box 728
Santa Fe, NM 87504-0728
(505) 988-6888
Web site: http://www.nps.gov/safe

Web Sites

Due to the changing nature of Internet links, the Rosen Publishing Group, Inc., has developed an online list of Web sites related to the subject of this book. This site is updated regularly. Please use this link to access the list:

http://www.rosenlinks.com/psah/meaw

OR FURTHER READING

Cantor, Carrie Nichols. *The Mexican War: How the U.S. Gained Its Western Lands.* Chanhassen, MN: Child's World, 2003.

Carey, Charles W., Jr. *The Mexican War: Mr. Polk's War.* Berkeley Heights, NJ: Enslow Publishers, 2002.

Collier, Christopher, and James Lincoln Collier. *Hispanic America, Texas, and the Mexican War, 1835-1850.* Tarrytown, NY: Benchmark Books, 1998.

Gaines, Ann Graham. *James Polk: Our Eleventh President.* Chanhassen, MN: Child's World, 2001.

Hoobler, Dorothy, and Thomas Hoobler. *The Mexican American Family Album.* New York: Oxford University Press, 1994.

Hunter, Amy Nicole. *The History of Mexico.* Broomhall, PA: Mason Crest Publishers, 2002.

Murphy, Jim. *Inside the Alamo.* New York: Delacorte Press, 2003.

 # BIBLIOGRAPHY

Chambers, John Whiteclay, II, ed. *The Oxford Companion to American Military History.* New York: Oxford University Press, 1999.

Christensen, Carol, and Thomas Christensen. *The U.S.-Mexican War.* San Francisco: Bay Books, 1998.

Eisenhower, John S. D. *So Far from God: The U.S. War with Mexico, 1846–1848.* New York: Random House, 1989.

Frazier, Donald S., ed. *The United States and Mexico at War: Nineteenth-Century Expansionism and Conflict.* New York: Macmillan Reference, 1998.

Johannsen, Robert W. *To the Halls of Montezuma: The Mexican War in the American Imagination.* New York: Oxford University Press, 1985.

Meyer, Michael C., and William H. Beezley. *The Oxford History of Mexico.* New York: Oxford University Press, 2000.

Winders, Richard Bruce. *Mr. Polk's Army: The American Military Experience in the Mexican War.* College Station, TX: Texas A&M University Press, 1997.

PRIMARY SOURCE IMAGE LIST

INDEX

About the Author

Liz Sonneborn is a writer and an editor living in Brooklyn, New York. A graduate of Swarthmore College, she has written more than forty books for children and adults, including *The American West*, *A to Z of American Women in the Performing Arts*, and *The New York Public Library's Amazing Native American History*, winner of a 2000 Parent's Choice Award.

Photo Credits

Cover, pp. 1, 14, 17, 32, 33, 34, 40, 43, 45, 52 Library of Congress Prints and Photographs Division; pp. 8, 12, 56 Library of Congress Geography and Map Division; pp. 10, 38 Texas State Library and Archives Commission; p. 12 © New-York Historical Society, New York /Bridgeman Art Library; p. 18 (left) Hulton/Archive/Getty Images; pp. 18 (right), 49 National Archives and Records Administration; p. 21 Library of Congress Manuscript Division; p. 24 The Society of California Pioneers; p. 26 General Research Division, The New York Public Library, Astor Lenox and Tilden Foundations: p. 27 (left) Missouri Historical Society, St. Louis; p. 28 (right) The Bancroft Library, University of California, Berkeley; pp. 29 (P-234), 54 (X-33833) Denver Public Library, Western History Collection; p. 47 © Randy Faris/Corbis

Designer: Nelson Sá; **Editor:** Christine Poolos;
Photo Researcher: Peter Tomlinson